Mottram

Parish

Church

A guide to the Parish Church of
Saint Michael and All Angels, Mottram-in-Longdendale
2001

Foreword
by the Bishop of Chester

The parish church of St Michael and All Angels at Mottram-in-Longdendale has stood as a beacon, visible for many miles, for centuries. Details of its original construction are lost in history, although like any living church it has been rebuilt and adorned with new monuments and furnishings over the years.

Many houses have been built within sight of the church, as the population has expanded. Amid all sorts of changes, Mottram Parish Church has stood as a symbol to the unchanging God who is worshipped here. Generations of people have cherished the building, as is evident from its fine condition as a new century begins.

I gladly pay tribute to all those who have cared for the church, and so lovingly produced this splendid guidebook. May all who come here be inspired to worship and prayer, and to service of the God in whose honour it was built.

† *Peter*

The Rt Revd Dr Peter Forster
Bishop of Chester and
Rector of Mottram Parish Church

Contents

'View of Mottram', taken from Aiken's '30 Miles Round Manchester', published in 1795
Engraved by E. Shirt

Introduction

"A large stately building of immemorial antiquity" - this was John Aiken's opinion of Mottram Church over 200 years ago . Who would describe it otherwise today?

This guide is an attempt to look into the past of this building, to look at the history of the stones and the furniture visible today and see what it can tell us. In doing this we encounter not just stones, but people - a rich variety of whom have worshipped in this building, worked for its maintenance, ordered and rearranged its furniture to suit their changing needs, stood up to the Mottram wind and who have found God meeting them within these walls.

The Guide is arranged such that visitors can take a tour around the Church, starting by the porch, proceeding down the South Aisle to the Staveley Chapel, looking at the Sanctuary, the Chancel, and returning via the Hollingworth Chapel, North Aisle and the Nave to the Tower at the west end of the Church.

The contents of the Guide are inevitably selective and only as accurate as present knowledge will allow, but we trust of interest to visitors to the church and to those seeking to discover their roots in Mottram parish.

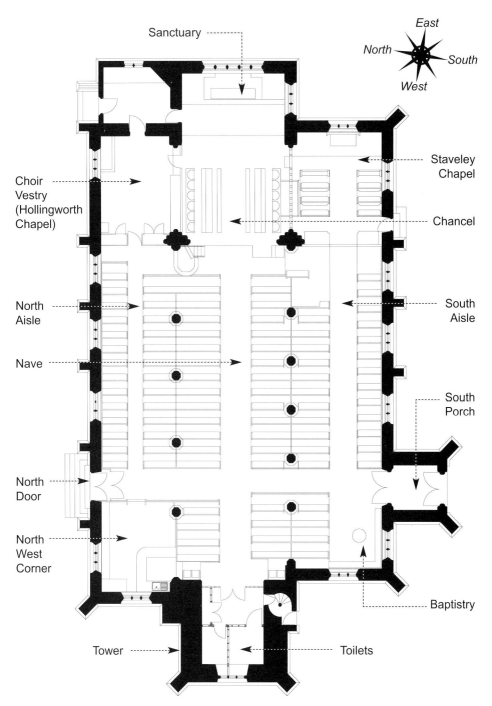

Plan of the church, 2001

5

South view of the church by Aiken, 1795

The changing face of the Parish Church

Recent research indicates that Mottram was the centre of a large Anglo Saxon estate. In 1066 it came into the ownership of the king, William the Conqueror, and by 1086 it had become part of the lands attached to the new Earldom of Chester. Mottram is mentioned in the Domesday Book but there is no reference to a church.

Evidence of a church at Mottram comes in the first quarter of the 13th century when clergy attached to Mottram church were witnesses to local documents. Later, in 1252, Robert, parson of Mottram, is recorded as being fined for helping poachers and in 1291 the church was mentioned in the papal taxation of that year.

Mottram's clergy were in those early days rectors, appointed by the lord of the manor through his 'right of advowson'. Many of the early rectors were absentee pluralists who held many benefices and left the work to local curates. On the creation of the new Diocese of Chester by Henry VIII in 1547 the bishop became rector, and still to the present day appoints vicars to run the parish on his behalf.

The early churches were estate churches, each built by the lord of the manor for himself and his tenants. They would have been small simple structures. There is little left here of any earlier building, only the Norman barrel font, the initials of a Hollingworth over the north door, the Decorated capital and the effigy of a knight and his lady in the Staveley chapel, and possibly the chancel arch.

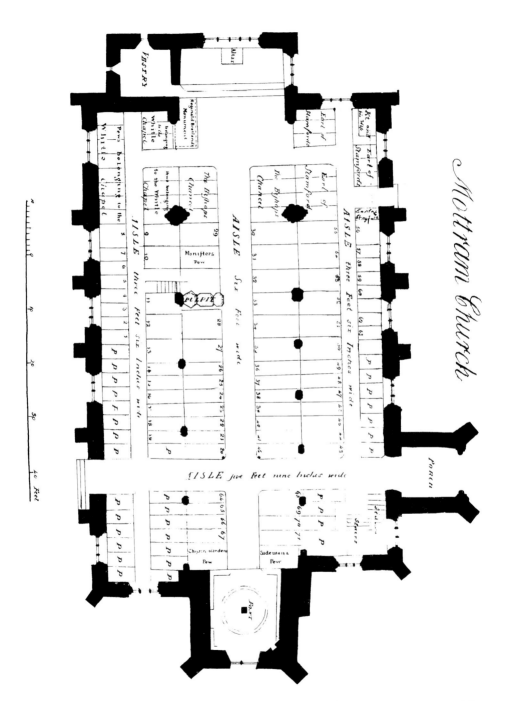

Plan of the church, dated 1820, showing the new pews, the font under the tower, a triple decker pulpit, and stairs to the galleries by the porch entrance.

View of the church soon after the 1855 restoration

The present church dates from the end of 15th century. It is built in the Perpendicular style with angled buttresses and castellated parapets. The building of the tower was supported by a bequest from Sir Edmund Shaa, a native of the area who rose to fame and fortune in London and died in 1488. It is possible that the whole of the outside walls were rebuilt at the same time, perhaps as an enlargement of the existing building.

In 1855 the church underwent a major restoration under the direction of local architect E.H. Shellard, during which the height of the nave roof was raised, allowing for much more imposing clerestory windows, and the vestry enlarged (compare the picture on page 6 with that above).

Apart from this, the structure of the Parish Church remains much as it was built some 500 years ago.

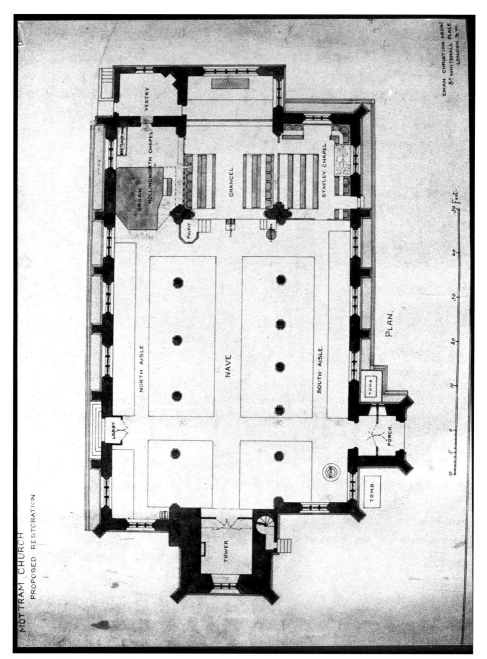

Plan of the church, (for proposed restoration in 1895), showing the rounded columns, the choir pews in the chancel, the font and pulpit in their present positions.

The South Porch

Standing in the porch the visitor can appreciate at once two factors which fundamentally affected the life of Mottram Church during the 19th Century. First, the reconstruction of 1855, which is commemorated above the church's main door in the following inscription:

The Pillars and Clerestory of this Church rebuilt
and the North and South aisles reroofed.
ANNO DOMINI MDCCCLV
The Revd. W. Henry Jones M.A. Vicar
Ralph Sidebottom
William Hardy Churchwardens

Second, for the visitor more interested in matters human than architectural, a glance at the west wall will show the plaque commemorating those members of the Sidebottom and Chapman families buried in the vault beneath the Porch. These two families intermarried and through their wealth, influence and dedication played a major role in the affairs of Mottram Parish for over 100 years along with many other industrialists, including the Daltons, the Rhodes and the Matleys. The Sidebottoms were active in the area from 1784 when they built their first mill; the Chapmans also made their money from textiles and later in the railway boom. The wording on the plaque shows, however, how all families, rich and poor, were in the last century affected by child mortality.

The Baptistry

The **font** is thought to be the oldest item of furniture to be found in the Church. It is a relic of the place of worship which stood here before the rebuilding of circa 1487. It is a 'barrel' or 'tub' font, hewn out of a single block, and probably dates back to the 12th Century.

For many years it was missing from its rightful place, put outside possibly by the Puritans in the 17th Century who disliked the Papal associations of the ancient font, or possibly later in Georgian times. John Wagstaffe, churchwarden in the early 20th century reports that "this ancient font was brought into the church by the Rev. W.H. Jones at the restoration of the nave in 1855. Up to that time it had served for many years as a water butt under one of the down-spouts on the south side of the church and the boys attending the old free school had been in the habit of washing their slates therein".

It now stands mounted on a millstone taken from the old Brightomley Mill at Hattersley village. The basin is lined with lead, and the font is covered by a heavy circular piece of iron-studded oak.

The 12th century barrel font

The **village war memorial** to the fallen of two World Wars is sited beneath the south window. This window, designed by James Powell & Son, portrays three English saints renowned for their prowess in battle, George, Oswald and Edwin. This window was placed here in 1921.

The window in the west wall commemorates Captain George Kershaw Sidebottom of the 5th Dragoon Guards, who died on board the Europa on his way home from the Crimea and was interred at Gibraltar on 23 July 1855 aged 24 years. Hence the window's watery theme of Jesus walking on the water and stilling the storm.

John Wagstaffe's oak coffer

The **oak coffer** to the right of the Sidebottom window introduces us to another family whose links with Mottram Church stretch back over centuries - the Wagstaffes. The initials on the coffer are those of the churchwardens of the day. A brass inscription tells us:

> *This Coffer belonging to the Parish of Mottram-in-Longdendale was replaced in this Church by John Wagstaffe 1906 - Warden*

The **clergy boards** recording the former rectors and vicars of Mottram were compiled by John Wagstaffe, churchwarden, and erected in 1904. The line of rectors goes back further than Jordan de Macclesfield, the first name on the boards, but we do not know for how long. Recent research however suggests that the parish and first church could have had their foundations before the Norman conquest in late Anglo-Saxon times. There is evidence of a 'Robert, parson of Mottram' witnessing a local document before 1225, and further references to a parson of Mottram occur in 1249, 1252 and 1291. So certainly there has been a Church on this site for some 800 years.

The South Aisle

The window at the eastern end of the south aisle is in memory of James Samuel Duckett, for two years churchwarden but, more importantly, for 52 years a member of the 'Organ Trust' which continues its benefactions to this day.

The Staveley Chapel

This chapel is said to have been originally dedicated to St. John, and was a chantry chapel belonging to the Staveley family. This means that the family would have employed a priest to say Mass daily in this chapel for both the living and the departed of the family. The **foliage patterned capital** in the Decorated style at the head of the column opposite the doorway, is unlike any other in the church, suggesting that this is one of the older elements of the building.

The two life-sized recumbent **stone effigies** on the north side of the chapel almost certainly represent Sir Ralph de Staveley (fl.1377 - 1419) and his wife Elizabeth. The knight's armour dates roughly from between 1390 and 1420. Both wear the 'S' collar awarded in recognition of loyalty and service to the House of Lancaster. It is known that Sir Ralph was a retainer of John of Gaunt Duke of Lancaster the son of King Edward III. The Lady Elizabeth may well have served in the household of the Duke or even of the King. The 'S' probably derives from the motto of the House of Lancaster - 'Souvent me souvient'.

The direct Staveley line ended in the 15th century with the death of Ralph Staveley (nephew of the above Ralph). By his will of 1456 he gave to Mottram Church 'my gold cross which I carry around my neck'.

The effigies are not in their original position. They were originally positioned against the south wall of the chapel. The effigies are carved from Derbyshire stone of a pinkish hue and have sadly been damaged over the years. Unusual features are the dog under the Lady's feet, and her wearing the 'S' collar.

The local legend of 'Sir Ro and his wife' linked Sir Ralph de Staveley to the Crusades of King Richard the Lionheart. Unfortunately this legend is some 200 years adrift. There was a crusade in Sir Ralph's time, but against the infidels of Lithuania in 1390, led by Henry Earl of Derby, later to become Henry IV.

Stone effigies of Sir Ralph and Lady Elizabeth Staveley

The chapel was privately owned until 1932. The last owners were the **Chapman family** who are fully commemorated in the window on the south side. The chapel came into their possession in 1857, purchased for £500 from the Earl of Stamford and Warrington, who once owned much land in the parish. The Chapmans guarded their private ownership jealously. This included the right to use the chapel's own private door, situated behind the curtain on the south side. This right was vigorously but unavailingly contested by the Reverend Henry Jones (vicar 1853-1878).

The chapel's east window was placed here by John Chapman as part of his refurbishment of the chapel in 1859, and depicts the Crucifixion.

The gift of the chapel to the church by the bequest of the late Mr Harold Chapman in 1932 is recorded on a tablet on the south wall.

The screens and furniture, including the **canopied seats** (some now placed at the west end of the church, some as clergy stalls in the chancel and some in the sanctuary), were provided by John Chapman in 1858. Most of the work was probably carried out by John and George Shaw, architects, of Uppermill, and was said to be copied from similar stalls in Lincoln Cathedral. The altar rail was made by Robert Thompson of Kilburn in Yorkshire, whose mouse trademark is carved into the base of the first right-hand newel post. The church mouse is still a popular attraction for young visitors to the church.

Up until 1935 the furniture was covered in a thick black paint. At this time it was cleaned and renovated by local craftsman Mr Harry Buckley during extensive alterations, leaving the chapel largely as we see today.

Harry Buckley, assisted by the Verger Stanley Roebuck,
at work cleaning the chapel screen, 1935

The chair by the altar has no ecclesiastical design on it, not surprisingly for it was one of a pair of fine **17th century dining chairs** from Hollingworth Hall. They were given to the church in 1831 by the Whitle family, at that time Masters of Hollingworth Hall, and, according to John Wagstaffe, were at that time used in the chancel as sanctuary chairs. The brass plaque commemorates this with the Latin words:

> *Deo et Sanctae Ecclesiae*
> *Rev^{dus} D. Whitle A.M. Oxon;*
> *de Hollingworth D^{mus}*
> *D.D.D. MDCCCXXXI*

17th century dining chair from Hollingworth Hall,
once used as a sanctuary chair

The **litany desk** is a memorial to Canon Michael Power, vicar from 1916 to 1951. Canon Power is still vividly remembered for his fiery sermons on Anniversary Sunday, delivered to a large crowd outside the church gates, often lambasting the local Council with his special brand of Irish humour.

The Chancel.

In former times, the chancel and sanctuary were areas reserved for the clergy and others with special connections to the Church. Now anyone can enter the chancel but the blue-carpeted sanctuary, where the bread and wine are prepared by the priest during Communion services, is still out of bounds to visitors.

Burials took place within the church until forbidden by Order in Council in 1861. One gravestone may be of interest here, that of William Coulborn, bearing the simple inscription:

> *WILLIAM COULBORN*
> *MINISTER BURIED*
> *JUNE THE 9*
> *1697*

He was vicar of Mottram for only two years, but legend has it that he had expressed the wish that he be buried standing up, hoping to get a head start on the rest in the journey to the Pearly Gates on the Day of Resurrection. Hence the small size of the gravestone. The gravestone has however clearly been reduced in size, probably to fit with the adjacent stones placed there in the 19th century. But it is a good story!

William Coulborn's gravestone

Another gravestone in the centre of the chancel is dedicated to the memory of

> **ROBERT HYDE**
> *of Catten Hall in the County*
> *of Chester*

This grandson of a Mottram vicar married into the wealthy Bretland family of Thorncliffe and on his death in 1684 was able to leave money to the Free School, and also to endow a charity 'to benefit the poor of the parish'.

John Wagstaffe reports that in 1868 the pews were removed from the chancel, new altar rails installed, the chancel roof repaired and new corbels fitted and plain choir stalls added. The present fine **oak choir stalls** were introduced in 1885 after considerable argument about the obstruction caused by their size. The faculty finally insisted that they be "not higher from the ground than 3' 8", the wooden floors being framed as moveable platforms laid down upon the paving, and the curbs all round being notched for ventilation".

The **chancel roof** is worthy of note, being of a great age. The beams however are pinned with rather large oak pegs, dating probably from the 1868 repairs.

The chancel roof, showing the c.15th oak timbers, pinned with c.19th pegs.

In the centre of the chancel the initials R.B. mark the place once occupied by the marble effigy of Reginald Bretland, who was buried there in 1703. The effigy was later moved to the north side of the chancel, and moved again in 1895 to its present position in the Hollingworth chapel.

The tombstone of Ralph Kinder (vicar 1779-1794) bears an interesting verse:

Ralph Kinder depd this life March 24th 1794 in his 59th year
When thus the Shepherd leaves his Flock
To mourn his absent Care
What Christian must not feel the Shock
And shed one genrous Tear?
But old and young alike must rise
And stand before the Throne
Nor should we weep when JESUS cries
To me ye blessed come
Contented rather let us smile
And bid our Griefs to cease.
Released from ev'ry Earthly toil
He's gone to rest in Peace.

The style of the **chancel arch** indicates that this could be another piece of an earlier church.

The **St Michael banner** was completed in 1983, being used for the first time in the Anniversary procession that year. It was embroidered by a team of parishioners to a design by Elizabeth Carrington. The whole took twelve months to complete and symbolises God's defeat of the powers of evil in the victory of Michael over the Devil as recorded in the Book of Revelation.

The St. Michael banner and the team that embroidered it
including Elizabeth Carrington (left).

19

The Sanctuary

The present **east window**, showing the Ascension of our Lord, was introduced in 1908 to commemorate Edward Chapman. The glazing which previously occupied this window now sits in the west arch.

View from the nave of the present east window, installed in 1908

The **south window** was given by Canon Miller (vicar 1878-1902) to commemorate Queen Victoria's Jubilee in 1887 and is one of the most beautiful in the church. It depicts the archangels of scripture, Michael (in the centre), Gabriel and Raphael (in the side lights). This window is the work of Hardman's of Birmingham, a long established and well known firm of church artists and furnishers.

Various clergy of the 19th century are commemorated on the wall tablets: William Johnson, James Turner, W. A. Pemberton and John Robert Charlesworth Miller. One notable omission is that of the Reverend W. Henry Jones, vicar for 25 years, under whose leadership the major restoration of the Church was undertaken in 1855. He was however, one of the few who did not die at Mottram but moved on to become vicar of Goddington, Oxford.

The **oak desk and seat** in the sanctuary are a memorial to Canon E. P. Tyson (vicar 1951-1956). He died very suddenly at the early age of 56, and his tomb is adjacent to the north wall of the churchyard.

The Choir Vestry (formerly the Hollingworth Chapel)

This was originally a chapel attached to the Manor of Hollingworth, hence the **stained glass coat-of-arms** of the various branches of the Hollingworth family placed in the north window by Captain de Holyngworthe who died in 1865. Private ownership appears to go back in a direct line to pre-Reformation days when this would have served as a chantry chapel for the Hollingworth family.

The replaced stonework near the door through the chancel screen, then the chapel's only door into the church, may indicate the position of the original piscina where the communion vessels were washed. The altar would have stood where the 'new' door now leads into the clergy vestry. Outside, a bricked-up window may be seen above the position of the door.

Canon Miller purchased the chapel in 1895 for the use of parishioners and especially for the new siting of the organ. The terms of sale insisted however on unrestricted access

Hollingworth coat of arms in the choir vestry window

being maintained to the main body of the church from the chapel. This meant leaving a narrow passageway past the organ to the north aisle and the organ console being sited to the rear. This left the organist out of direct view of the choir and congregation and overwhelmed by his own instrument.

When the new organ was purchased in 1998 and placed in the south aisle, the space was reordered for use as the choir vestry and meeting room.

Over the north door (looking from outside the church) can be seen, carved in stone, a **coat of arms** bearing three holly leaves, thought to be that of John Hollingworth. Judging from the style of the letters and the fact that the size of the stone does not match the surrounding stone coursework, this may be a remnant of a much earlier building, possibly dating back to the early 13th century.

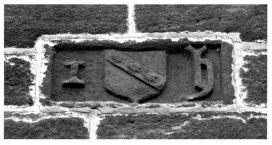

The Hollingworth coat of arms over the north door

Next to the window in the choir vestry is the **Bretland memorial.** This monument was originally placed in the centre of the chancel where there is now a commemorative stone. It was moved first to near the doorway of the Hollingworth chapel and in 1895 to its present position in the chapel.

The Bretland family were minor freeholders in Hollingworth from around 1408. Reginald's father John, an eminent lawyer, was a colourful and outspoken opponent of the Puritans of the area who held sway in Mottram Church between 1643 and 1662. Their Hollingworth estates were seized by the Parliamentary government in 1647 during the Civil Wars, but were returned in 1654.

Reginald Bretland is dressed in the gown and scarlet hood of a Sergeant-at-Law in the classic pose of the philosopher. Sergeant-at-Law was the highest order of barrister in England and Ireland until the abolition of the order in 1873. He was Master of Thorncliffe Hall in the village of Hollingworth and acquired a large amount of property not only in Hollingworth but in Werneth and Romiley and in Lancashire and Derbyshire.

Reginald Bretland's memorial

The Latin translates as follows:

Here lies buried
Whatever was mortal
of REGINALD BRETLAND, Serjeant-at-Law,
Descended from an honourable family:
Illustrious in Virtue, in Learning, in Genius,
Who,
Prudent in deliberating, eloquent in speaking, resolute in acting,
Anxious for peace, avoiding litigation, faithful in the highest degree
to his clients,
Managed the affairs of others committed to his charge as diligently
as his own,
Nor ever preferred instituting a lawsuit to removing the cause of
controversy.
No day passed by him unemployed.
At last, satiated with life,
His soul, replete with virtues, deserving well of his country,
He peacefully surrendered to God on the third day of April, in the
year of our Lord 1703,
In the 62nd year of his age.
Let us labour incessantly.

On a slight thread depend man's transient joys;
With sudden lapse his firmest hopes decay;
Time while we speak, on envious pinion flies.
Snatch the swift hour nor trust a future day.

(the verse at the end is from Horace, Ode 5, Book 1)

The North Aisle

The window at the eastern end is the most recent in the church, being installed in 1996. It incorporates stained glass that was removed from the west window at the base of the tower. This had originally been put there in 1857 "in affectionate memory of John and Arminal Reddish by Joshua their son" and depicted Jesus, the succour of the needy, giving bread and drink and supporting the lame.

The new window replaced a vandalised window in memory of William Johnson (vicar 1826-1840). William Johnson was already 56 when he became vicar of Mottram. He remained for 14 years until his death at the age of 71. His son (as the plaque on the window sill tells us) became a canon of Manchester Cathedral.

A tablet commemorates the restoration of the north aisle seats in memory of Thomas Cresswell Harrop, Sunday School teacher, who died in 1899.

The **north door** is not used today, but of note are the **bread racks** to either side. On their shelves were placed loaves baked specially for distribution to the poor of the Parish. The racks are inscribed:

> *The Gift of Dame Elizabeth Booth to the Poore of this Parish for*
> *Ever. Anno 1619*

> *The Gift of Mrs. Margaret Booth of Wooley to the Poore of this*
> *Parrish for Ever 1737.*

These racks were used until the middle of the 20th century. At one time they were situated on the south wall, in 1904 they were repaired and placed at either side of the door into the tower, and at another time they were fixed on the pillars next to the cross aisle.

Dame Elizabeth Booth was the widow of Sir William Booth of Dunham Massey. The Booths owned considerable estates, especially in Cheshire, including the manors of Hattersley and Staley, and therefore the Staveley chapel. The Booth crest, we are told in 1662, was painted on the wall of the chapel. In her will, Dame Elizabeth left gifts for the poor of various parishes - Great Budworth, Bowdon, Wilmslow, Mottram and Ashton-under-Lyne. Her gift to Mottram was for £2-10s-0d per annum, "to be distributed in bread every Sunday for ever". The gift of Margaret Booth of Wooley was for £2-12s-0d per annum, "to be distributed in weekly loaves for ever" and paid out of an estate in Honley, Yorkshire.

Mottram Parish Charities, with whom the money is now vested, still distributes its annual income to needy elderly people in the area. The charity is presently administered by the churchwardens.

The **benefactors board** listing donations to the church, to Woodhead Chapel and to the Free School, was put up in 1904 and used to be flanked by another which read as follows:

Benefactors to the Poor of the Parish of Mottram

1748	*William Tetlaw, of Godley, gave for ye use of ye Communion one Silver Chalice, Value*	*£10*
1763	*Thos. Heginbotham, of Mottram, gave for the use of ye Communion one Silver Chalice, Value*	*£30*
	To the Poor	
1743	*Thos. Sidebotham of Staley*	*£5*
1760	*John Hadfield, of Croden-brooke, Longden*	*£20*
1763	*John Booth, of Woolley, in Hollingworth gave*	*£40*
1801	*Mary Wagstaffe gave*	*£60*
1806	*Agnes Wagstaffe gave*	*£50*

The pews were removed from the **north west corner** in 1982 to make space for a social area. In 2000 this was greatly improved by the installation of a kitchenette, which has proved of great benefit to the congregation and visitors to the church.

At the west end of the aisle, the "Ruth" window in memory of Frank Ingham came from St George's Old Church, Stalybridge. On its closure, at the wish of his widow, the window was brought to Mottram and installed in 1970. The window depicts the story from Ruth, Chapter 1.

The bread racks

The Organ

Congregations were increasing in the 18th century, so much so that in 1704 a gallery was built along the south wall to provide extra seating, and another at the west end in 1753. In those days the congregation was led by the Mottram Singers and a band of a trumpet, kettle drums and a bassoon, all seated in the west gallery.

By 1819, in the days of James Turner (vicar 1794-1826), the need for an organ was acute. A public subscription list was raised and an instrument was purchased. It was built by George England and sold by Edward Foster of Greek Street, Soho, London. It stood in the west gallery, the back of which was open to the tower. As the public subscription exceeded the cost by some £300, this money was used for the purchase of land in Hollingworth known as Long Croft. The income from the development of this land was to be used for the repair and maintenance of the organ, the payment of an organist and the furtherance of the church's work generally. Hence the building of the Organ Inn and row of adjacent cottages on Hollingworth Market Street (in those days known as Treacle Street) and also the formation of the 'Organ Trust' to disburse the income. The Trust continues its beneficent work today, including an annual grant to the Parish Church choir.

The south gallery was demolished during the 1855 restoration followed, in 1895, by the demolition of the west gallery. The organ was removed to the Hollingworth chapel and much enlarged. It had been regarded as a very fine instrument, but by 1997 its condition was such that repairs and continuing maintenance were out of the question. Reluctantly the Church Council decided to replace it.

A new organ was purchased in 1998 from Makins of Oldham. This fine three-manual electric instrument owes its authentic voice to the computerised sampling of real organ pipes. The new console is much more conveniently placed in the south aisle, and the sound comes from powerful speakers concealed behind the single row of old organ pipes situated over a new screen at the eastern end of the north aisle.

The gallery at the west end of the nave, showing the organ in its original position, gas lighting and the first set of pews.

The old pipe organ in its 20th century home in the Hollingworth chapel

The candelabrum

The Nave

The nave roof was raised to its present height in the restoration of 1855. The original roof-line can be seen in the stonework high on the tower wall above the west arch. Much needed repair work all around the building was done at that time, and this can be identified in many places as patches of newer stone.

The **painted boards** above the chancel arch display the three traditional pillars of Christian faith and life - The Creed, The Lord's Prayer and the Ten Commandments. The paintings represent Moses and Aaron (lawgiver and father of the Jewish priesthood). Legend attributes the painting of these boards to a travelling artist who presented them to the church in return for hospitality.

The boards were formerly attached to the east wall of the church as a reredos, whilst on the chancel arch were displayed, so a record of 1633 tells us, the Royal coat-of-arms flanked by the coats-of-arms of the Booths of Dunham Massey (Lords of the Manors of Staley and Hattersley), and the Wilbrahams of Woodhey (Lords of Longdendale). Thus the faithful were reminded not simply of God, their Lord Spiritual, but equally forcibly of their Lordships Temporal. The royal and manorial coats-of-arms were removed in 1879 by Canon Miller shortly after his arrival.

The **pulpit** is made of the finest alabaster with six full length figures standing in niches at the angles and six intricately traceried panels portraying some of the most famous biblical preachers together with incidents from their lives. The sculptor was Harry Hems of Exeter who worked to a design by Messrs Weaver and Adye, architects of Devizes and Bradford-on-Avon. A brass tablet records the gift of the pulpit:

> *To the glory of God and in the memory of Edwin Hugh Shellard of Old Hall, Mottram; Born 8th February 1815, at rest 1st February 1885. This pulpit is dedicated by his widow.*

Shellard was a noted church architect, especially in the North West, and it was he who had overseen the restoration of the church in 1855.

The oak **eagle lectern** was given by Edward Chapman as a memorial to his father John Chapman who died on 18th July 1877 and is commemorated in an inscription at the base of the pedestal which concludes "Thy word is a lantern to my feet", a reminder of the importance of the Lectern as the place from where the bible is read during church services.

Pews were first installed in 1817/18 to replace the forms and benches that were then the only seating for the congregation. The new pews were to be rented, and a rental sale took place on 16th Sept 1818. These pews were replaced in the 1890's by the ones you see today with their fine carved oak ends. Wood from the old pews was reused in the making of the new pew backs.

The alabaster pulpit

The **candelabrum** is inscribed around its bottom bowl:

John Harrison, Vicar,
Daniel Wooley and John Dewsnap, Churchwardens A. D. 1755

Canon Miller wanted to place the candelabrum in the chancel when gas lighting was introduced to the church in 1885, and included this in one of his numerous faculty petitions. He was however thwarted in this instance by the Chancellor of the Diocese by whom 'faculties' have to be granted for such changes. The Chancellor took note of the feelings of Parishioners, who were opposed to this change.

The former east window, in its present position in the west arch screen

The **west arch screen** was erected by private donation in 1896 after the removal of the organ and west gallery. The dedication reads as follows:

> *This screen was erected to the glory of God by Mrs Elizabeth Colston to the memory of her great-grandparents, William and Betty Lees of Newton and of their descendants interred in this Church and Churchyard. A.D. 1896*

The screen was dedicated on Mottram's great occasion of the year, the afternoon service of the Sunday School Anniversary, 5 June 1896, "in the presence of a large congregation".

The space above was originally left open but was filled in with clear glass in 1901 to keep out draughts. The clear glass was later replaced with the original east window, which had been erected over the altar in 1857 by John and Ann Chapman in memory of George Sidebottom of Hill End, the father of Ann and uncle of John. It was altered to fit in the west arch screen and was placed there on 18 December 1913 by George John Chapman, grandson of George Sidebottom.

Either side of the arch can be seen the **scare-devil figurehead corbels,** one of which was an original feature of the 15th century building. The right hand corbel is clearly a later reproduction.

The Tower

The exact date of the building of the tower is uncertain. What is certain is that money was left for its erection in the will of **Sir Edmund Shaa** (Shaw), Royal Jeweller under Edward IV, Richard III and Henry VII. Edmund and his brother Ralph were born in the Mottram district, of Dukinfield parents. Ralph also became famous as an Austin friar and, with Edmund, was active in establishing Richard III on the throne. Edmund became Mayor of London and member of the Goldsmith's Company.

Edmund bequeathed 40 marks (1 mark = 13s-4d or 67p) to Mottram Church "to be spent on the making of the steeple.... if it be not made at my decease" and the same amount for St Mary's Church in Stockport. He founded Stockport Grammar School and left money for the building of a chapel at Woodhead, now the Church of St James. Sir Edmund died on 20 April 1488. It is possible that when the tower was built more money was found, thus enabling the rebuilding of all the external walls.

Much of the stonework clearly dates from this period and comes from quarries on nearby Tintwistle Moor (Tinsel Knarr). This stone is as exposed to wind and weather on its hilltop site as any in the County and yet the preservation of the gargoyle faces around the parapet indicates its durability.

The tower accommodates four storeys - a room at ground level housing the toilets, above which are the ringing chamber, the clock chamber and the belfry itself. Below is a basement, formerly used as a charnel house, where bones from re-used graves were stored. It is possible to gain access to the roof using a vertical ladder past the bells, from where, given suitable weather (which can be a rare phenomenon), extensive views may be had over North Cheshire, Greater Manchester and the Derbyshire Peak District.

Unusual is the fact that Mottram Church has no west door at the foot of the tower, the reason being, no doubt, the sharp fall of the land here. The position of the present church may have been dictated by earlier, perhaps smaller, churches on this site.

The scare-devil corbels either side of the west arch

Before the restoration of 1855 the **ground floor of the tower** was open to the nave, and plans of the church in 1820 show a large font sited centrally there. The west gallery above was reached by a staircase in the south aisle.

When the organ was moved to the Hollingworth Chapel in 1895 the base of the tower was enclosed by the new west arch screen.

In the year 2000 the ground floor room, which had since 1984 been used as the choir vestry, was fitted out with toilets including facilities for the disabled and for baby changing. The stained glass from the west window, now the toilet window, had been removed in anticipation of this work and incorporated into a new window at the eastern end of the north aisle.

The narrow door on the left gives access to a spiral staircase leading up the tower. For some years this door was blocked up to prevent bell-ringers who had drunk too much ale from coming straight into church. The door was discovered and reopened in 1896.

To the left of this door may be seen a surviving piece of the 19th century pews, with brass plates still affixed to its panels recording the identity of the parishioners who had rented them.

The record breaking team of bell ringers, 1906

The **ringing chamber** bears a plaque on the walls describing the work of 1885 when gas lighting was introduced and the bells were rehung.

> *St Michael's Church*
> *Gas introduced*
> *Bells rehung and quartered*
> *Two treble bells renewed*
> *By public effort 1885*
> *The Revd J R C Miller, M A Vicar*

It comes as no surprise that there is no tablet to record the event three years later in December 1888, when the ringers resigned "en bloc" and the bells ceased to ring. The cause, it seems, was the cessation of payments to the ringers for their work. In past years they had been paid very handsomely but Canon Miller, ever sensitive to spiritual issues, wrote in the magazine:

"It should be understood that the work of a Church Bell Ringer is a religious office, as is that of any other Church officer, and there seems to be no reason why its duties should not be discharged as a labour of love for the sake of the Church as is the case with the Choirmen."

A new team, it seems, was soon recruited and achieved such skill in the art of change ringing that a remarkable record was established, which is commemorated on another plaque fixed to the north wall:

> *Chester Diocese Guild of Bell-ringers*
> *In this tower was rung*
> *on June 8th, 1906*
> *E Timbrell's Peal - Kent Treble Bob Major*
> *16,800 changes in 9 hours 40 minutes*
> *This is the longest length yet rung in the method*
> *Revd W A Pemberton Vicar*
> *John Wagstaffe*
> *T M Whittingslow Wardens*

Three years later the bells again were silenced. The ringers complained that the frame was unsafe and needed replacement. Some months later a generous donation in memory of Henry Gartside of Thorncliffe Hall, from his brothers Edmund and John and sister Ruth, enabled the re-casting and re-hanging of the bells to go ahead. Messrs Taylor & Co. of Loughborough undertook the work and on 10 September 1910 the new bells were dedicated by the Bishop of Chester.

View of the tower and the hearse house from the
churchwardens' steps

Above the ringing chamber is the **clock chamber.** The clock mechanism is
Mottram's third clock. The first, dating from 1761 or possibly earlier, was replaced
in 1791. This second clock ground to a halt in 1937 and was not replaced until 1952
when a much younger clock, made originally in 1878 by J.B Joyce for Ardern Park
in Bredbury, was installed. In 2000 the clock and its two faces were restored and a
new electric winder fitted as part of Tameside MBC's millennium celebrations.

In the **belfry** above the clock chamber hang the bells on their steel frame. The bells
have a long history. In 1548 a Commission reported that Mottram-in-Longdendale
had "ij white chalices and a rynge of iij belles". The metal of these old bells is still
contained in those which now hang in the tower.

In 1723 Abraham Rudhall of Gloucester accepted the contract to "cast the three
old bells into five good new tuneable bells". The cost was £141-13-0. The following
year another bell was cast to complete the set of six. The transport of bells from
Gloucester to Mottram in those days, before the building of canals or railways, was
no easy task. They travelled by barge up the River Severn to Shrewsbury and were
there collected by horse drawn waggon from Mottram.

In 1805 two treble bells were added. These two new bells however proved unsatisfactory and in the re-hanging of 1885, undertaken by Messrs Mears and Stainbank, these two were recast and the whole peal retuned. Each bell is inscribed to record the recastings, including the latest one in 1910 by John Taylor & Co. of Loughborough. The inscriptions are as follows:

Treble	*Hora Fugit Ora Church of St Michael*
	(J.R.1805, M & S 1885) J.T. & Co 1910
2	*Our voices shall with joyful sound*
	Make hill and valley echo round
	(J.R. 1805, M &. S 1885) J.T. & Co 1910
3	*Prosperity to the Parish of Mottram-in-Longdendale*
	(A.R. 1723) J.T. & Co 1910
4	*W A Pemberton, Vicar*
	(A.R. 1723) J.T. & Co 1910
5	*John Wagstaffe & T M Whittingslow, Ch. Wardens*
	(A.R 1723) J.T. & Co 1910
6	*Peace and good neighbourhood*
	(A.R. 1723) J.T. & Co 1910
7	*The peal was recast and hung in a new frame by John,*
	Edmund and Ruth Gartside, in memory of their brother Henry
	Gartside, who died March 10th 1909
	(A.R 1723) J.T. & Co 1910
Tenor	*I to the church the living call, and to the grave do summon all*
	(A.R 1723) Johannes Taylor et Socii, Loughborough, Omnes
	Fecerunt Anno Domini 1910

The new bells outside the church in 1910 , waiting to be hung.

The Churchyard

This would have once looked very different, being just a small area bordering the church, with its headstones standing in serried ranks. A plan drawn up by John Sidebottom in 1798 shows a small building, marked as Thomas Shaw's house, where the present gates stand, the main path leaving the churchyard just to the west of the house. On 23rd March 1818 the churchwardens gave notice to all who had headstones in the churchyard to agree to have them laid flat. At about the same time Thomas Shaw's house was demolished.

The churchyard extension, shown on the plan, was consecrated in December 1827. Most burials in those days took place in churchyards but by the mid 19th century many of them, like that at Mottram, were full. From 30th March 1842 till 15th April 1843 the sexton, James Cooper, dug graves for 242 burials. There are 1322 marked graves and a number which have no headstone. Some record just one burial, others as many as nine or ten. At an average of four each, there must have been some 6,000 bodies interred in the churchyard in the 250 years from the middle of the 17th century to the end of the 19th. The number buried in the previous 400 years will never be known, although the parish registers will give some idea for the last 100 years of this period.

An additional burial ground was acquired in 1858. This was to be kept permanently separate and apart from the churchyard. It was administered first by the Burial Board made up of ratepayers elected by the parish, then by Mottram Urban District Council, and now by Tameside MBC.

The Memorial Garden for the burial of ashes was consecrated in 1987.

To the left of the path from the main gates, the visitor will find the Millennium Yew. A cutting was taken from the 2,000 year old Gwytherin Yew in Wales, and planted here in November 1999. Further along on the right is the oldest recorded grave in the churchyard, dated 1649 and inscribed with the initials AC and A9 (April 9th?).

Continuing clockwise round the church, stop and admire the bellringer's tombstone at the head of the churchwardens steps, a memorial to a man much missed by his fellow bellringers.

To the north east of the church, the grave of Lewis Brierley tells a chilling tale of a tomb emptied by grave robbers in 1827:

> *Tho once beneath the ground his corpse was laid*
> *For use of surgeons it was thence convey'd.*
> *Vain was the scheme to hide the impious theft*
> *The body taken, shroud and coffin left.*
> *Ye wretches who pursue this barb'rous trade*
> *Your corpses in turn may be convey'd*
> *Like his to some unfeeling surgeons room*
> *Nor can they justly meet a better doom.*

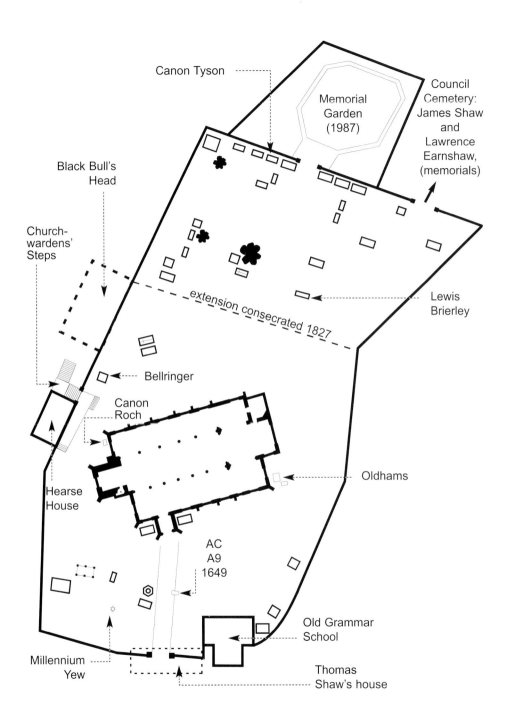

Plan of the churchyard

37

There are three more 'musical' graves. Firstly, towards the north west corner of the graveyard, that of James Shaw for whom there is a much larger memorial in the council cemetery. Decorated with musical instruments, the memorial bears words and music from the Messiah, which was performed at a concert to raise funds for its erection. Along the east wall of the church lie the Oldham family, two of their gravestones bear witness to their great love of music.

Lawrence Earnshaw, well known locally for his inventions, including an astronomical clock, is buried in an unmarked grave in the churchyard, but his memorial is to be found in the Council Cemetery, the tallest monument there in fact. However, the artist L.S. Lowry, who lived and worked in Mottram, was not buried here, but at Manchester's Southern Cemetery.

The **Old Grammar School,** or Mottram Free School as it was properly called, is situated next to the main entrance to the churchyard, and is now a private residence, having been sold in 1996 to finance the toilets and kitchenette in church.

There is evidence of a school at Mottram from as early as 1570, but the Mottram Free School was founded in 1619 by two benefactors, Robert Garsett, an alderman of Norwich, and Sir Richard Wilbraham, the Lord of Longdendale, who each gave £100 to its foundation. This was during the long incumbency of John Hyde who was vicar for 62 years. The first Schoolmaster to be appointed was John Etchells, who remained in post through all the troubles of the Civil War and Commonwealth until his death in 1670 aged 88 years. The post was then taken over by the vicar, at that time Henry Moreton (vicar 1662-1676).

The Old Grammar School

By the end of the 18th century the school had become much dilapidated and in 1836 was described as being in a ruinous condition. In 1858 the long overdue reconstruction took place, which is commemorated in the Latin inscription on the west wall. The present building is a much larger building than the original. Although the Grammar School closed in 1912 the building continued in use for educational purposes even after the building of the 'new' Grammar School nearby, now Mottram C.E. Primary School. In the 1960's it was still used as an overflow classroom.

The **hearse house** was built originally in 1775 to house the hearse which was provided by the church for use at funerals. This use ceased in the 19th century, when firms of undertakers began to appear. The building became dilapidated, and was demolished and rebuilt in 1895. After this it was used as a library and young men's club, until dampness forced them out. The upper floor was later used for a time as the mortuary for Longdendale U.D.C.

The steps to one side are known as the **churchwardens' steps** as a number of them are commemorated in the stonework.

The derelict building at the bottom of the Churchwardens' steps was the old **Black Bull's Head.** It was built in 1769 and closed in 1911. The pub is famous for its 'Body Snatchers Watch', established after the theft of Lewis Brierley's body from the graveyard. Now only a false front remains. Some archaeological excavation and tidying of the site took place in 1999. There are plans to continue this work.

The hearse house

Extracts from the Registers

In 1538 Thomas Cromwell, Vicar General to Henry VIII, issued a mandate ordering every parish priest to keep a record of all baptisms, marriages and burials which took place within his parish. The record was to be kept in a strong lockable chest bought for the purpose, and new entries were to be entered up each Sunday after service. These early registers were frequently kept on loose sheets of paper which were easily lost or damaged, and this may have happened to the early Mottram records.

In 1598 Queen Elizabeth I ordered that all these old records were to be transcribed into parchment books, especially those dating from the start of her reign in 1558. The first register still survives, and opens with the following:

> *A true and perfect register off all Christeninges Burialls and*
> *Weddinges in the p(ar)ish of Mottram since the begining of hir*
> *M(a)je(sty) 's Raine accordinge to the ould Ancient Booke of the*
> *same p(ar) ish as here followes.*

The book begins with baptisms, the first being that of **Andrew Handforth** on March 26 1562. Weddings and burials start in 1559 with the marriage of **George Greenes and Joane Carlill** on November 9th and the burial of **Adam Eliot** on December 8th. Up to the 1590's the entries are simply a list of names, and then gradually more details are included; the father's name at baptisms and the place of residence, be it township or farm. Certain entries are in John Hyde's own hand such as the burial of **Hamnet Hyde my sonn** on January 3 1617. Hamnet Hyde had been to London in 1610 to be cured by the touch of King James of 'The Kings Evil' (tuberculosis of the lymph glands), and this is noted on a spare page in the marriage register.

John Hyde was buried on March 17 1636 after being vicar for 62 years, and within a few years the civil wars between king and parliament erupted. The confusion shows itself in the registers. The vicar Gerard Brown was ejected in 1643, and between 1646 and 1652 the register is badly kept: in 1649 no baptisms were recorded, in 1650 only 4 burials were noted, dates were omitted and details were entered haphazardly. Between 1647 and April 1651 no marriages were recorded, and other records show that Mottram people went to neighbouring parishes like Glossop to be married. There is also a gap in marriage entries between 1658 and 1662.

In 1653, Parliament under Oliver Cromwell ruled that custody of parish registers and the right to marry people was to be taken from the parish priest and given to a lay Registrar. This lasted until the restoration of Charles 11 in 1660. Although the registers were better kept during this period, the number of marriages celebrated at Mottram fell sharply.

The burial registers record a number of violent deaths like these poor souls:

> *23/6/1610 Robert Newton de parish of Glossop slayne in the Marle*
> *pitt of John Harrop of Mottram.*

> *17/4/1615 A poore man from Richards Shepley's w(hi)ch hee hadd*
> *unchristianly delte withall att the firste in laying him in a hoale by*
> *the high waye syde.*

The above entry was also recorded for some unknown reason in code:

> *1 p4492 718 f947 richi9de sh2p623s ...*

During the 17th century illegitimate births were recorded in detail since the parish, responsible for such children, wanted to make sure of its liability. For example:

> *6/2/1620 Edward base sonn of Ellyn Cynder who will not confesse*
> *the father thereof*

> *8/12/1632 Edward s.o. Jane Hilton of the parish of Worsley in the*
> *county of Lancaster & the supposed father is Mr. Frances Ratcliffe*
> *dwelling at Ordsall.*

In 1678, with the intention of boosting the wool trade, a law was declared that henceforth all corpses were to be buried in a woollen shroud. The Mottram burials register records that in August 1678

> *Grace dau of Mr. Wilkinson de Semanthy in Derbyshire and Sarah*
> *Harrison deMatley... Both yt were first buryed in Woll at Mottram*
> *Ch(urch).*

Fears that registration would be used to raise taxes were realised in 1694 when charges were introduced and used to fund the wars against France. Costs were 2/- (10p) for baptisms, 2/6 (12.5p) for weddings and 4/- (20p) for burials.

The law regarding marriages had been flouted for some time, and in 1754 Hardwicke's Act called for a separate register for marriages, with printed pages. Banns were to be called and the register was to be signed by the participants. The first marriage in the new book at Mottram was in April 1754. Baptisms and burials continued in the old book until 1813 when Rose's Act ordered that three separate books of printed forms should be used and that extra details like age and parents' names should be included.

In 1837 when civil registration was introduced, birth, marriage and death replaced baptism, marriage and burial in the official record. However, the parish registers still record these three religious events at Mottram as they have done for over 400 years.

A Historical Cross Reference

c.1225 Local deed indicates a church at Mottram served by 'Robert, parson of Mottram'.	**1215** Magna Carta. **1291** Last of the crusades in the Holy Land.
c.1420 Death of Sir Ralph de Staveley.	**1415** Battle of Agincourt.
c.1488 Building of the Tower and probable rebuilding of the exterior. Woodhead Chapel also built at this time.	**1492** Christopher Columbus discovers the Americas.
1547 Transfer of patronage of Mottram Church from the Crown to the Bishop of Chester. Nicholas Hyde, first vicar of Mottram, was inducted.	**1547** Death of Henry VIII. **1599** Spanish Armada.
1619 Foundation of Mottram Free School.	**1605** The Gunpowder Plot.
1643 Ejection of Gerard Browne, vicar, for royalist sympathies and his replacement by Parliamentarian Preachers.	**1640-1648** English Civil War. **1665** Newton discovers gravity.
1688 Act of Toleration, allowing licences to be granted for several Nonconformist Chapels in the area.	**1685** Birth of George Frederick Handel. **1692** Salem Witchcraft Trials in America.
1753 West Gallery built. **1761** First clock installed in the tower.	**1776** American Declaration of Independence. **1789-1848** French Revolution.
1855 Church restoration and raising of the Nave roof.	**1854** Florence Nightingale organises a group of nurses to go to the Crimean War.
1888 Building of St Mary Magdalene Church, Broadbottom.	**1885** Karl Benz makes the first motor car. The first Kodak box camera on sale.
1910 New bells hung in the tower.	**1914-1918** World War I - the war to end all wars.
1951 New clock installed in the tower.	**1939-1945** World War II.
2000 Toilets installed in the tower. A major restoration scheme planned.	**2000** The start of the third Millennium celebrated by Christians the world over.

Further Information

Those who are interested in Mottram's long line of vicars and rectors, going back to the 13th century, should read *The Parish of Mottram-in-Longdendale and its Clergy* by Canon Richard Price, author of the first edition of this guide. Visitors wishing to know more about the story of the schools in the parish are directed to *Schooldays in Mottram Parish*, edited by Rev. A.J. Rees. Both these books are on sale in the Church.

For those who are researching their family history it should be noted that only the most recent parish registers are actually held locally, and enquiries about these should be addressed to:

The Vicarage, 29 Ashworth Lane, Mottram, Hyde, Cheshire, SK14 6NT tel 01457 762268

The records listed below are available on microfilm and microfiche at:

Tameside Local Studies Library, Astley Cheetham Public Library, Trinity Street, Stalybridge, Cheshire SK15 2BN. tel 0161 303 7937   fax 0161 303 8289 email localstudies.library@mail.tameside.gov.uk

banns	1830-1844
baptisms	1562-1975
burials	1559-1988
burials index	1802-1988
marriages	1559-1948

The originals of these and other records can be viewed also on microfilm at:

Cheshire and Chester Archives and Local Studies, Cheshire Record Office, Duke Street, Chester, CH1 1RL. tel 01244 602574   fax 01244 603812 email recordoffice@cheshire.gov.uk website http://www.cheshire.gov.uk/recoff/home.htm

Indexes of births, marriages and deaths from the General Register Office for the years 1837 to 1970, are available on microfilm at:

The Greater Manchester County Record Office, 56 Marshall Street, New Cross, Manchester M4 5FU. tel 0161 832 5284   fax 0161 839 3808 email archives@gmcro.co.uk website http://www.gmcro.co.uk

The Longdendale valley, as seen from the Memorial Garden